PIANO SOLO

MORE SUNDAY SOLOS FOR PIANO

PRELUDES

2   Agnus Dei

5   Come, Christians, Join to Sing

10   Come, Thou Fount of Every Blessing

14   Doxology

17   For the Beauty of the Earth

20   The Heart of Worship

24   How Great Thou Art

32   How Majestic Is Your Name

29   Shout to the Lord

36   Sweet, Sweet Spirit

OFFERTORIES

40   Amazing Grace

43   El Shaddai

46   Fairest Lord Jesus

50   God Will Make a Way

54   Great Is Thy Faithfulness

58   His Eye Is on the Sparrow

62   O God, Our Help in Ages Past

64   Thy Word

70   Turn Your Eyes Upon Jesus

67   We Fall Down

POSTLUDES

74   All Hail King Jesus

82   The Ash Grove (Let All Things Now Living)

77   God of Grace and God of Glory

88   Immortal, Invisible

91   Joyful, Joyful, We Adore Thee

110   Lift High the Cross

94   Mighty Is Our God

98   O Magnify the Lord

102   O Worship the King

106   Praise to the Lord, the Almighty

Note: Many of these arrangements are appropriate for more than one category.

ISBN 978-1-4234-7372-5

HAL•LEONARD®
CORPORATION
7777 W. BLUEMOUND RD. P.O. BOX 13819 MILWAUKEE, WI 53213

Visit Hal Leonard Online at
www.halleonard.com

AGNUS DEI

Words and Music by
MICHAEL W. SMITH

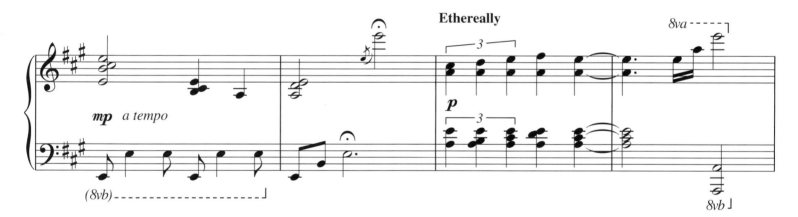

COME, CHRISTIANS, JOIN TO SING

Words by CHRISTIAN HENRY BATEMAN
Traditional Spanish Melody

Moderately fast

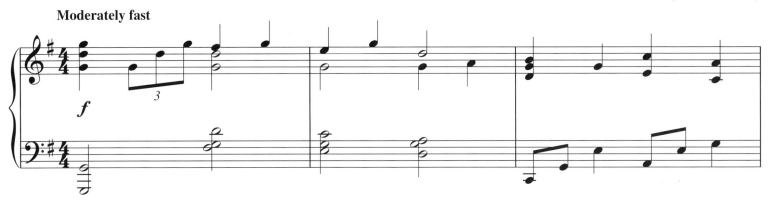

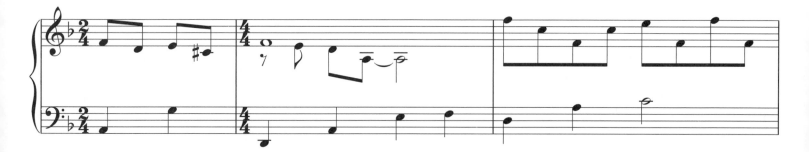

cresc.

Slower

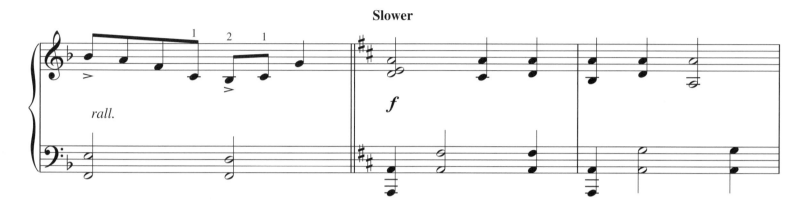

rall.

_f_

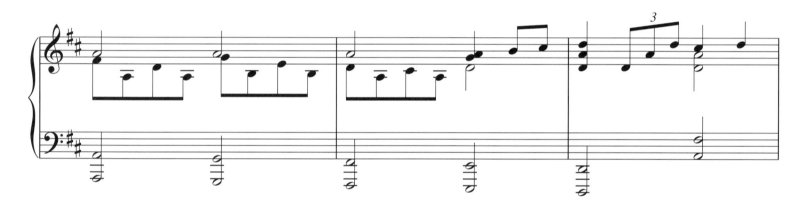

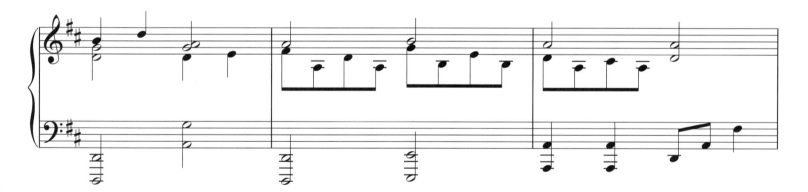

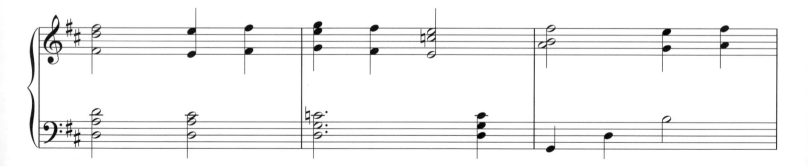

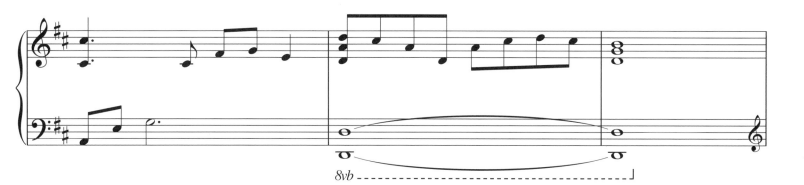

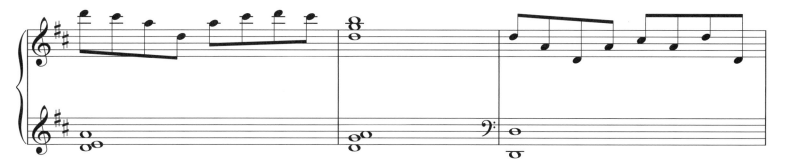

molto rit.

8vb

COME, THOU FOUNT
OF EVERY BLESSING

Words by ROBERT ROBINSON
Music from *The Sacred Harp*

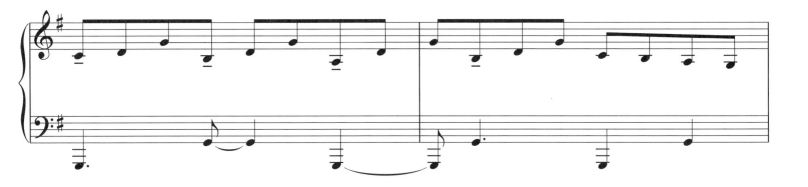

13

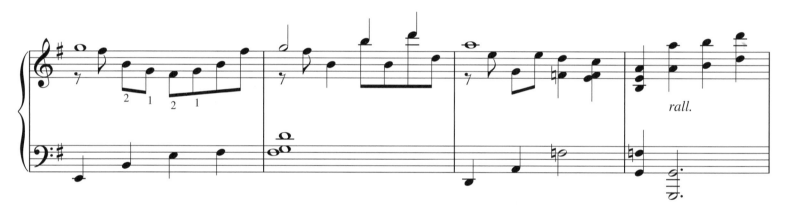

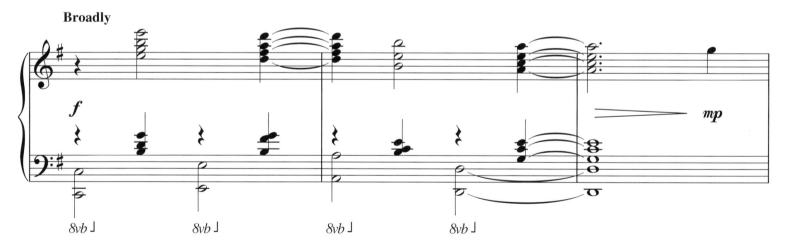

DOXOLOGY

Traditional

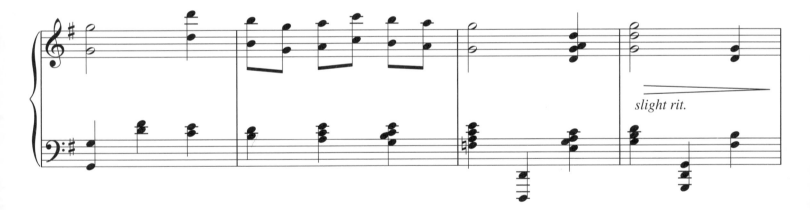

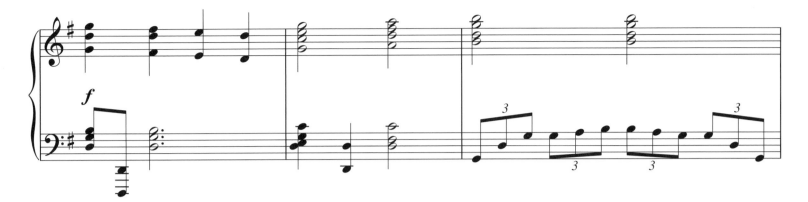

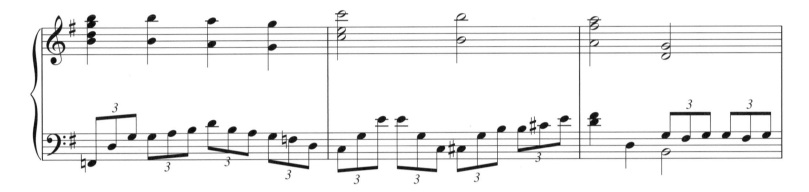

FOR THE BEAUTY OF THE EARTH

Words by FOLLIOT S. PIERPOINT
Music by CONRAD KOCHER

Stately

THE HEART OF WORSHIP

Words and Music by
MATT REDMAN

Steady Ballad

mp

With pedal

mf

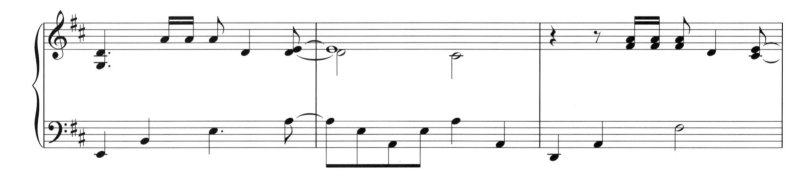

HOW GREAT THOU ART

Words and Music by
STUART K. HINE

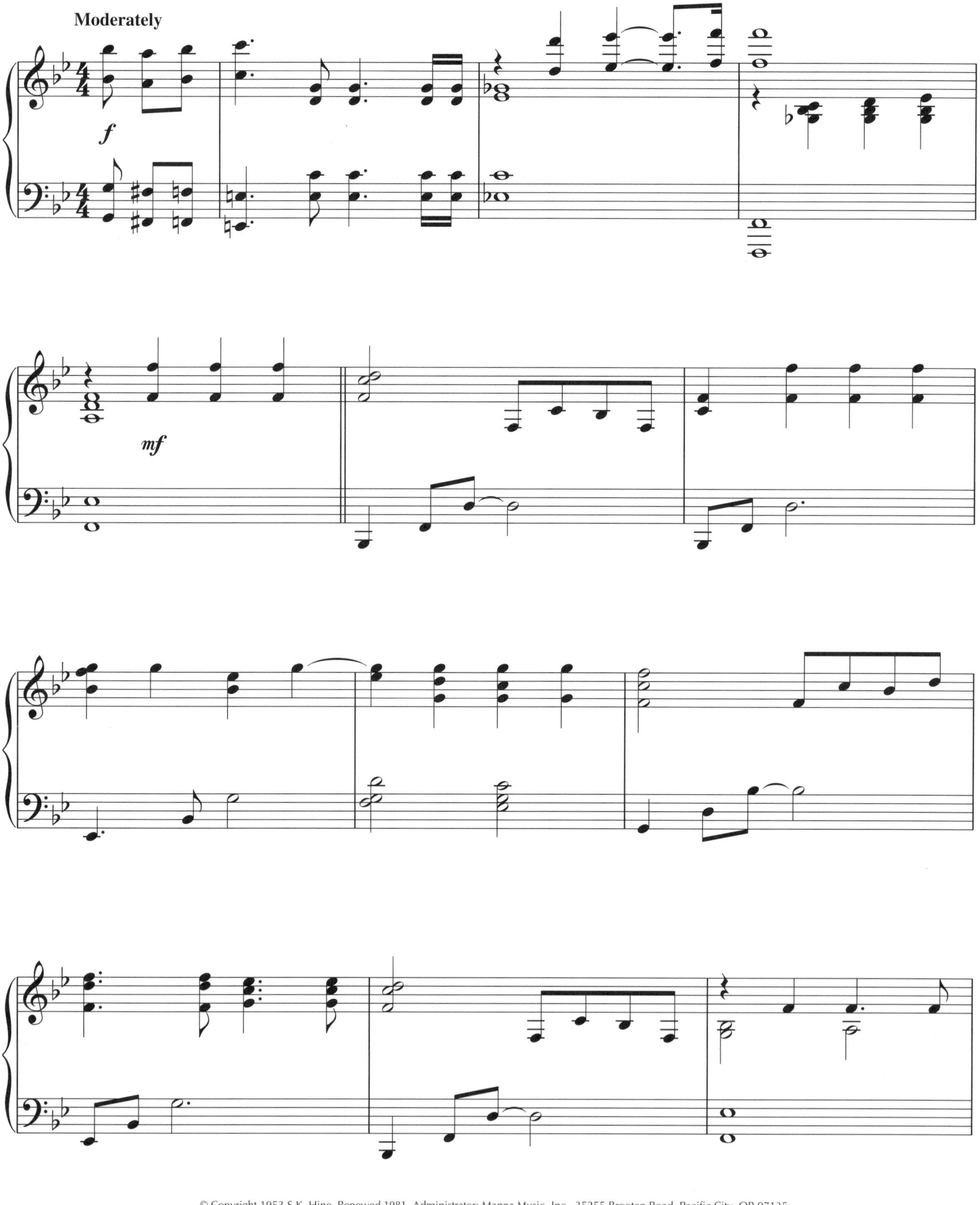

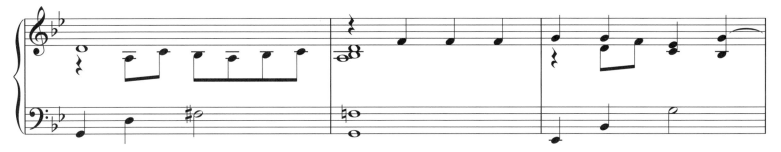

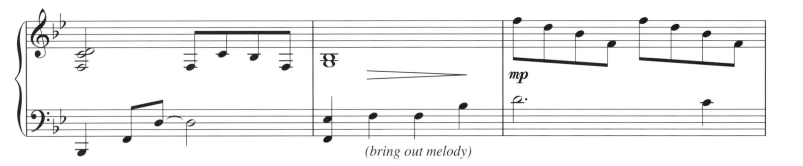

(bring out melody)

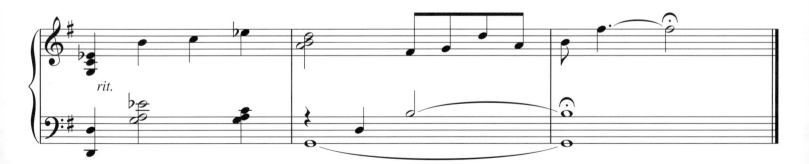

SHOUT TO THE LORD

Words and Music by
DARLENE ZSCHECH

D.S. al Coda

CODA

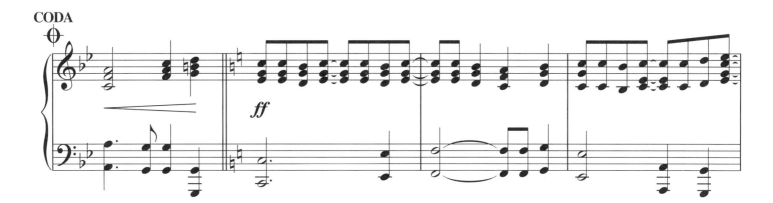

HOW MAJESTIC IS YOUR NAME

Words and Music by
MICHAEL W. SMITH

Majestically, in 2

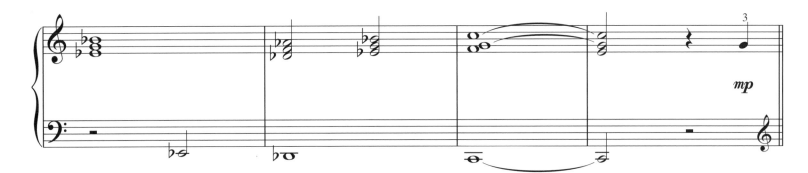

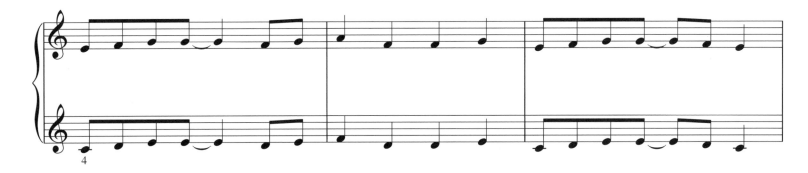

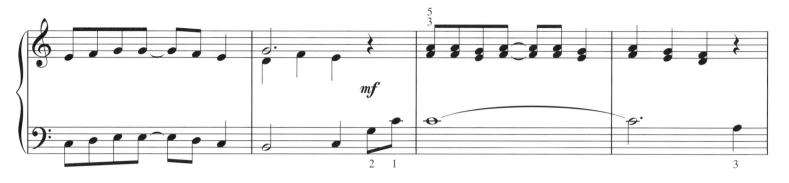

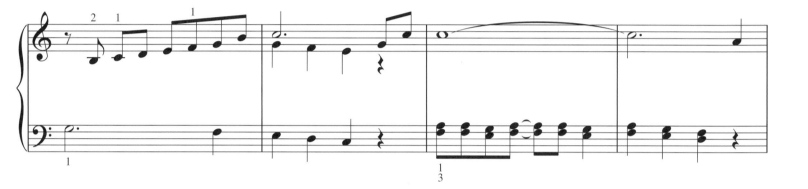

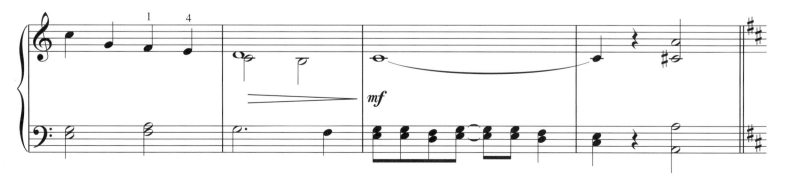

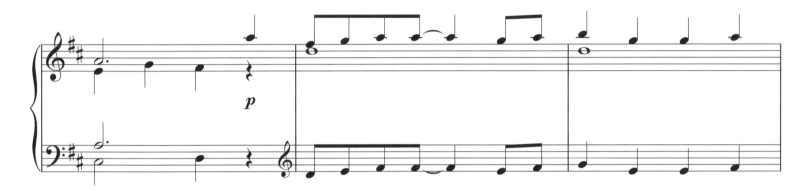

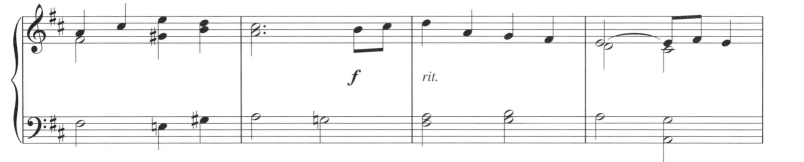

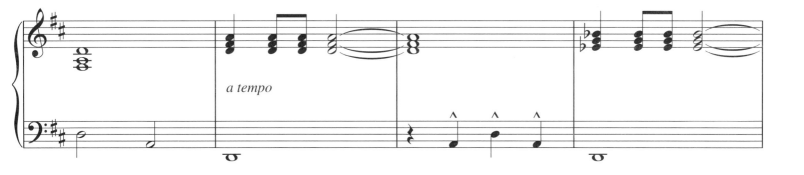

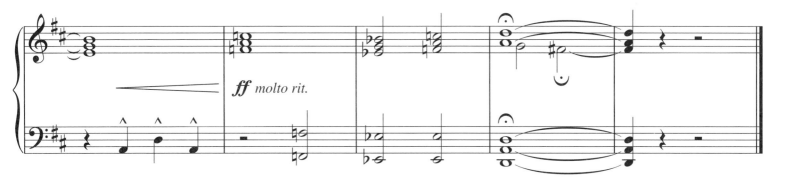

SWEET, SWEET SPIRIT

By DORIS AKERS

Gently

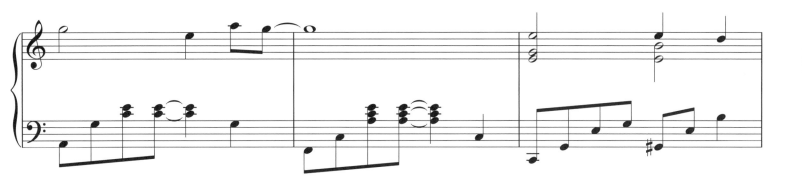

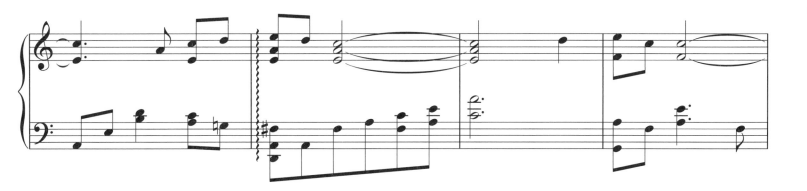

AMAZING GRACE

Words by JOHN NEWTON
Traditional American Melody

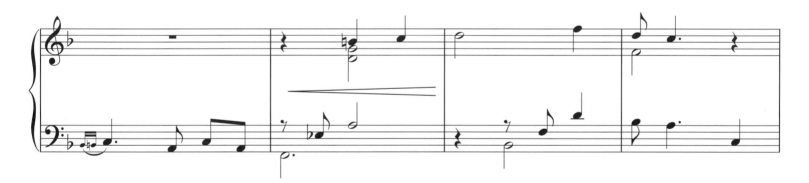

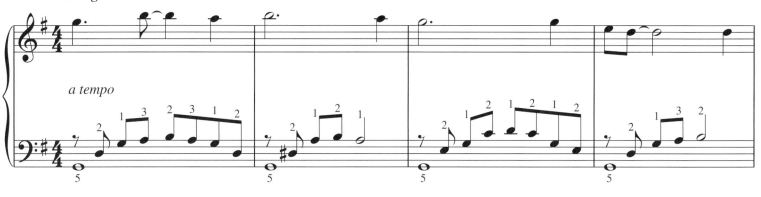

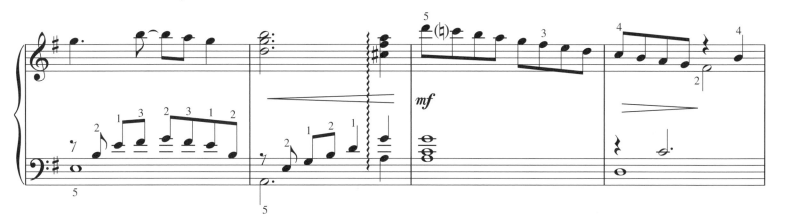

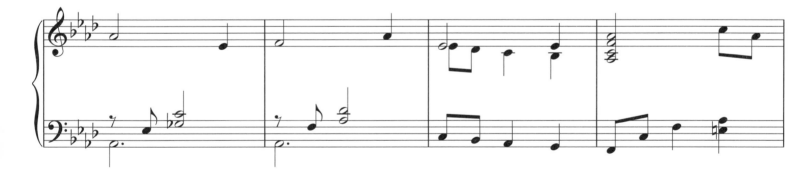

EL SHADDAI

Words and Music by MICHAEL CARD
and JOHN THOMPSON

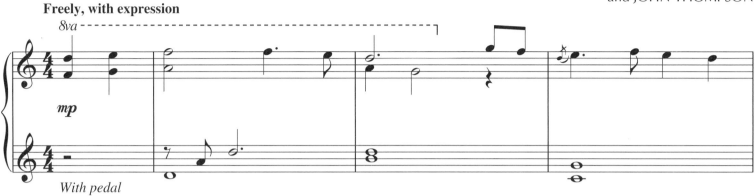

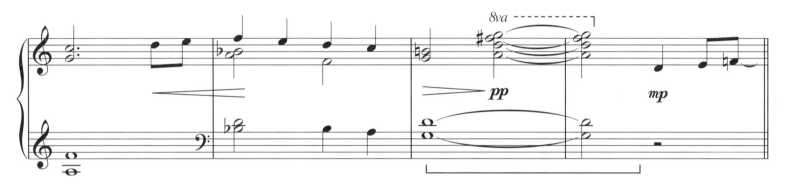

To Coda ⊕

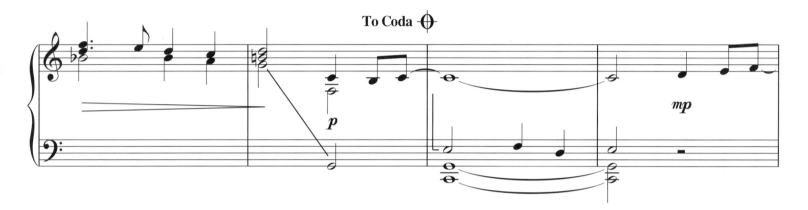

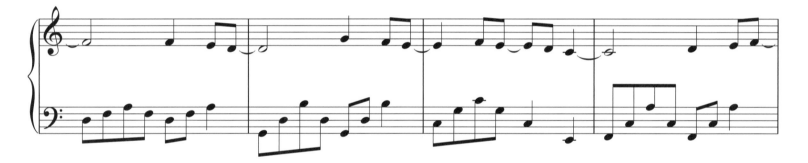

FAIREST LORD JESUS

Words from *Münster Gesangbuch*
Verse 4 by Joseph A. Seiss
Music from *Schlesische Volkslieder*
Arranged by RICHARD STORRS WILLIS

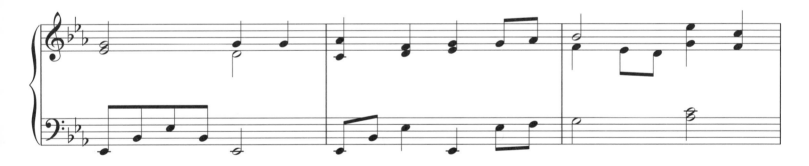

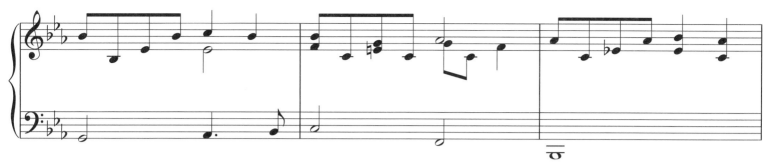

GOD WILL MAKE A WAY

Words and Music by
DON MOEN

Moderately

cresc. poco a poco

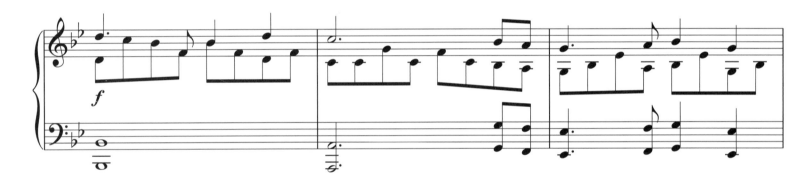

f

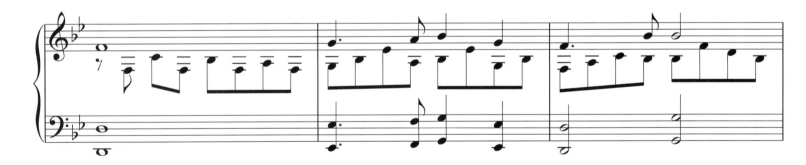

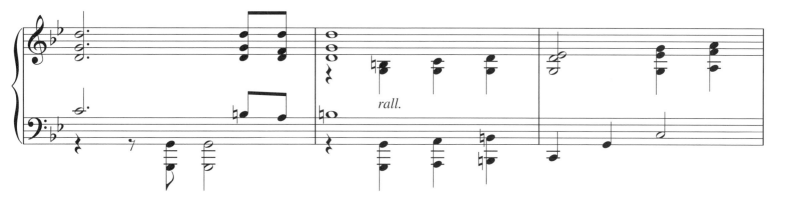

GREAT IS THY FAITHFULNESS

Words by THOMAS O. CHISHOLM
Music by WILLIAM M. RUNYAN

Rubato, with much feeling

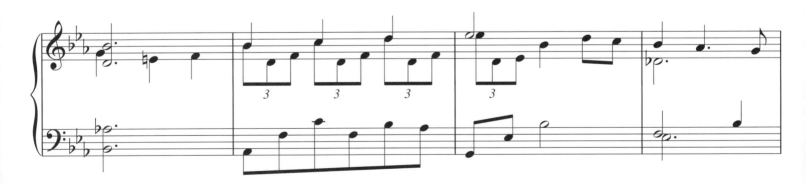

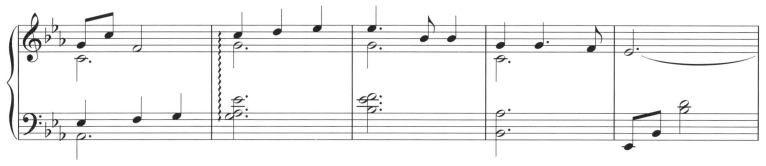

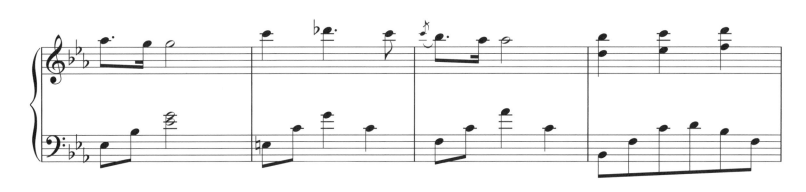

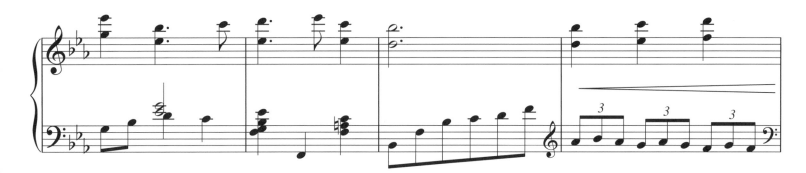

cresc. poco a poco

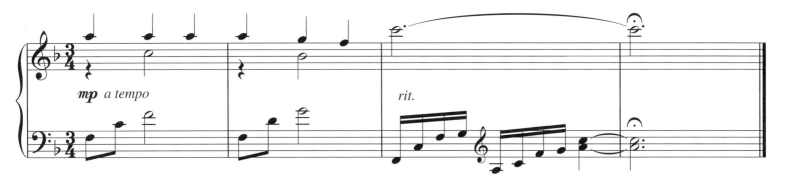

HIS EYE IS ON THE SPARROW

Words by CIVILLA D. MARTIN
Music by CHARLES H. GABRIEL

Freely

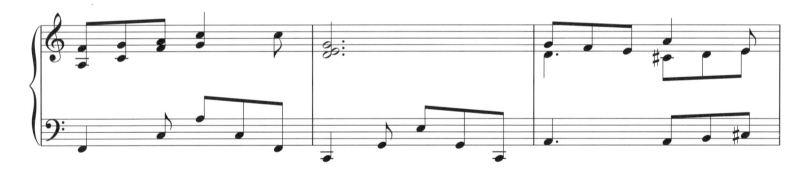

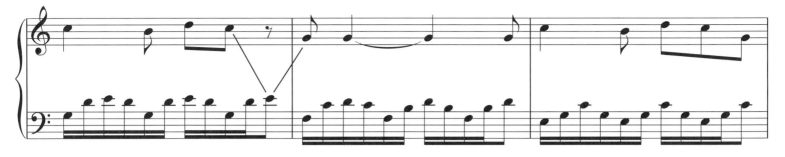

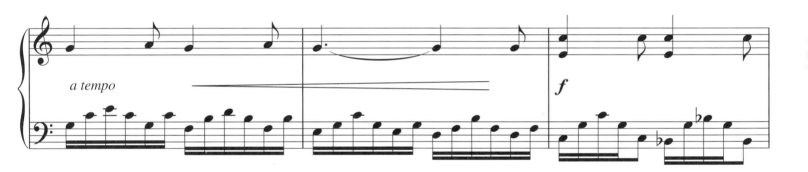

O GOD, OUR HELP IN AGES PAST

Words by ISAAC WATTS
Music by WILLIAM CROFT

With simple elegance

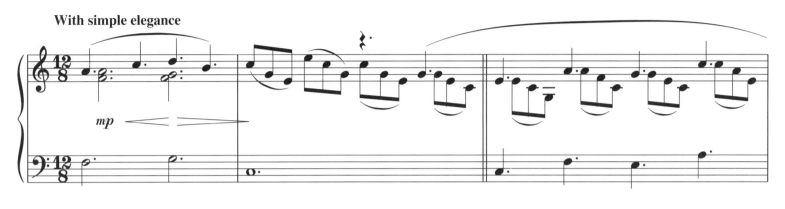

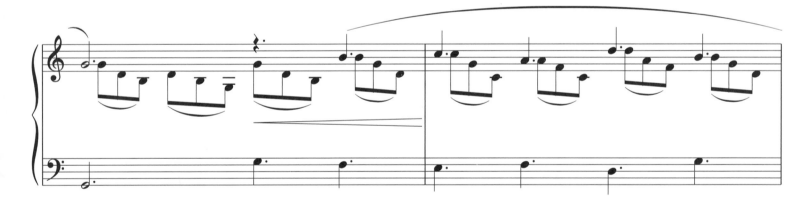

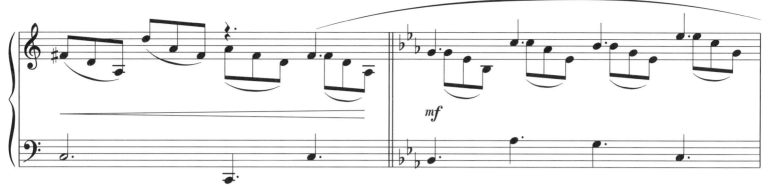

THY WORD

Words and Music by MICHAEL W. SMITH
and AMY GRANT

WE FALL DOWN

Words and Music by
CHRIS TOMLIN

Worshipfully

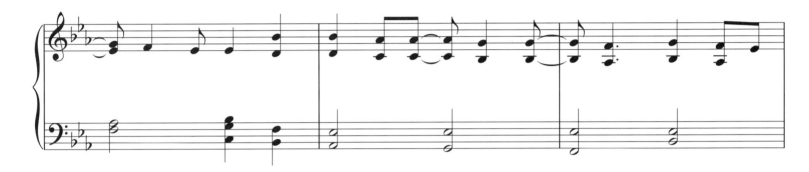

TURN YOUR EYES UPON JESUS

Words and Music by
HELEN H. LEMMEL

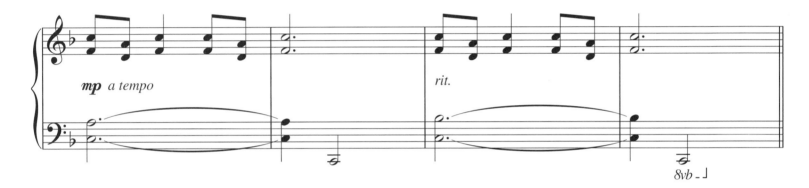

Delicately

a tempo

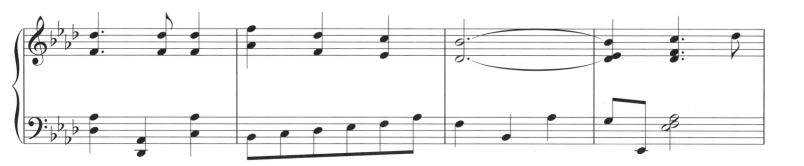

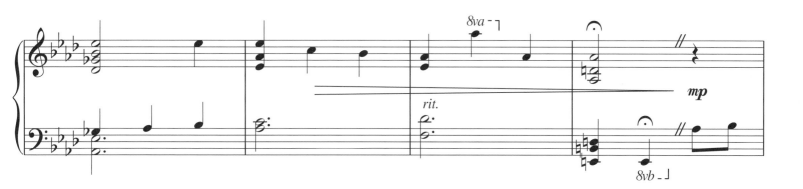

ALL HAIL KING JESUS

Words and Music by
DAVE MOODY

Majestically

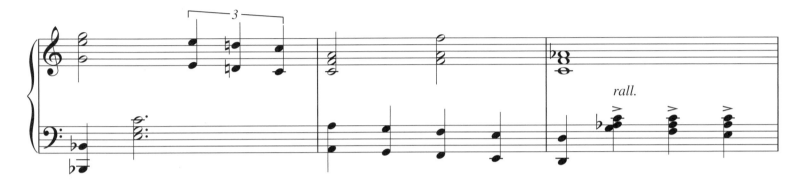

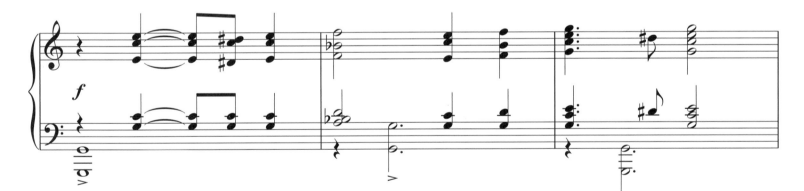

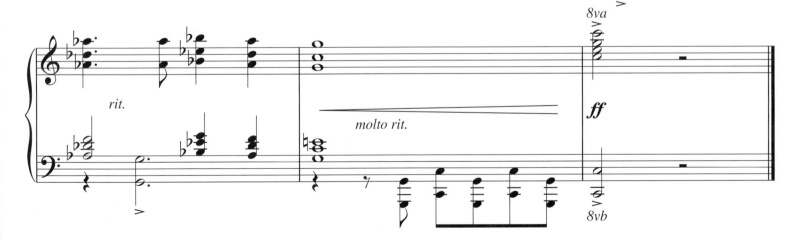

GOD OF GRACE
AND GOD OF GLORY

Words by HARRY EMERSON FOSDICK
Music by JOHN HUGHES

Stately

With energy

THE ASH GROVE
(Let All Things Now Living)

Traditional Welsh Air

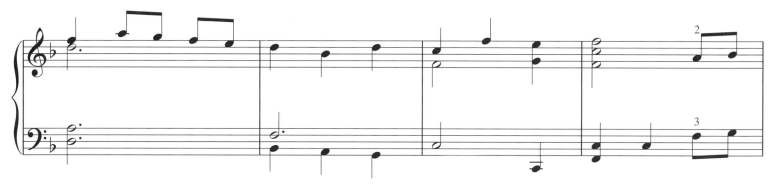

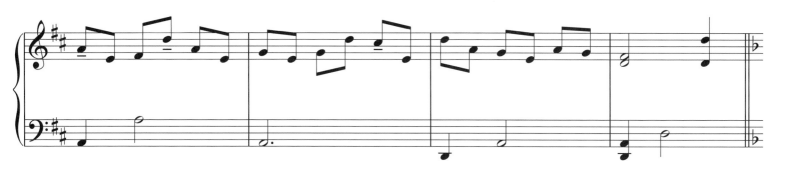

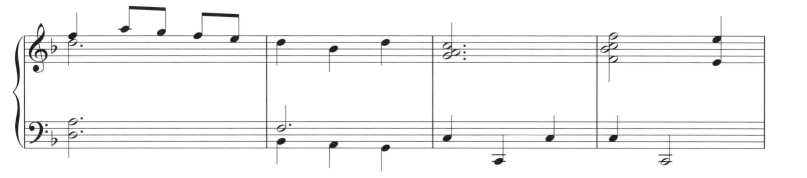

IMMORTAL, INVISIBLE

Words by WALTER CHALMERS SMITH
Traditional Welsh Melody
From John Roberts' *Canaidau y Cyssegr*

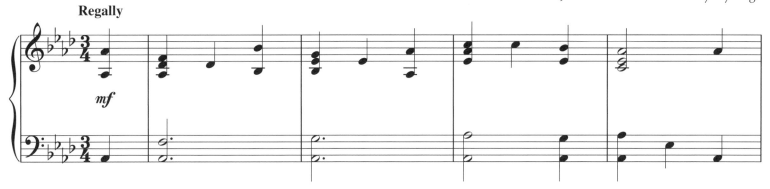

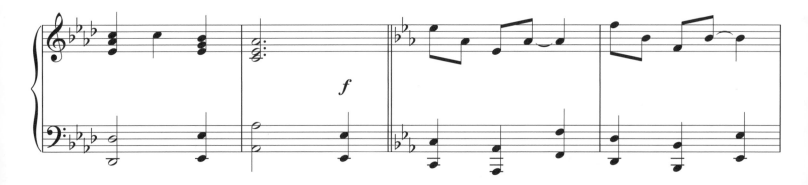

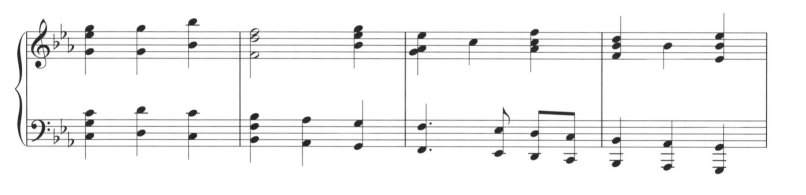

JOYFUL, JOYFUL, WE ADORE THEE

Words by HENRY VAN DYKE
Music by LUDWIG VAN BEETHOVEN,
melody from *Ninth Symphony*
Adapted by EDWARD HODGES

Brightly

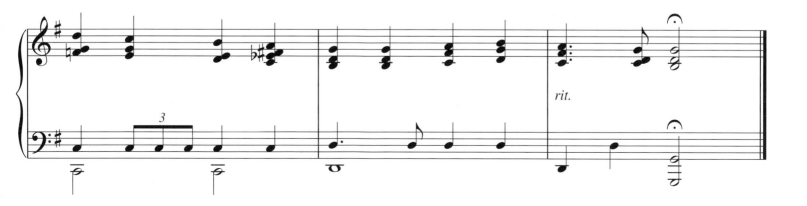

MIGHTY IS OUR GOD

Words and Music by EUGENE GRECO,
GERRIT GUSTAFSON and DON MOEN

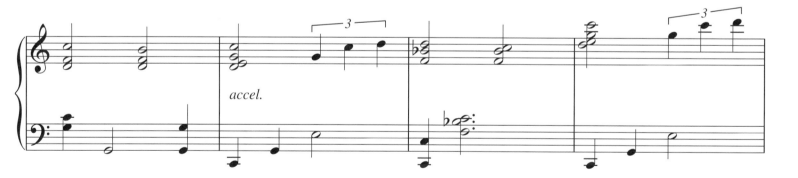

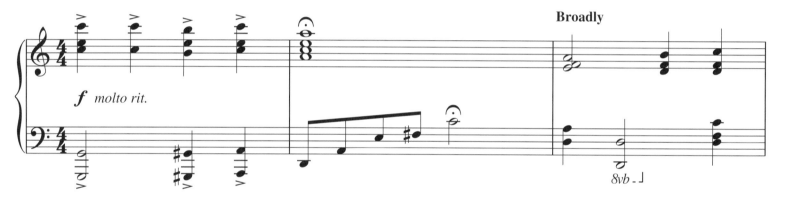

O MAGNIFY THE LORD

Words and Music by MELODIE TUNNEY
and DICK TUNNEY

O WORSHIP THE KING

Words by ROBERT GRANT
Music attributed to JOHANN MICHAEL HAYDN
Arranged by WILLIAM GARDINER

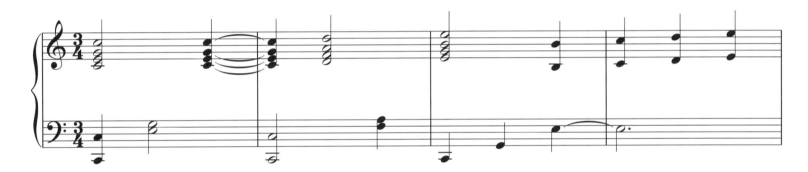

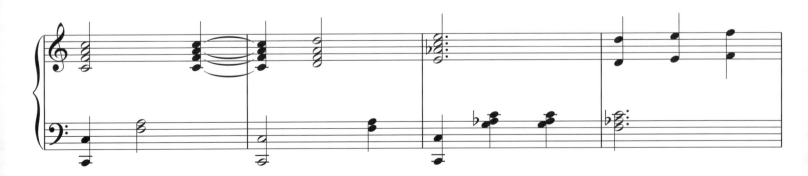

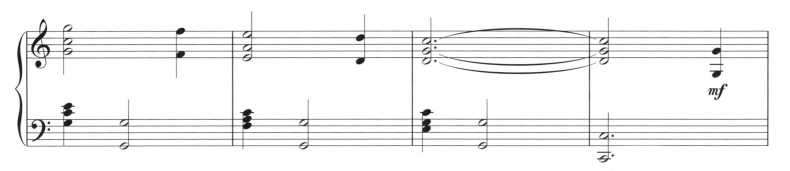

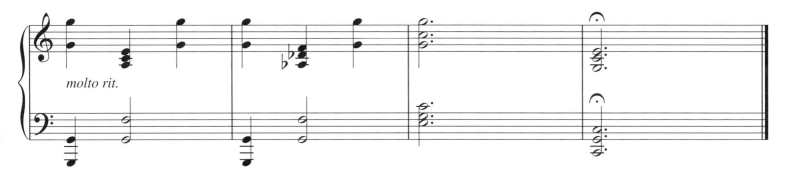

PRAISE TO THE LORD, THE ALMIGHTY

Words by JOACHIM NEANDER
Translated by CATHERINE WINKWORTH
Music from *Erneuerten Gesangbuch*

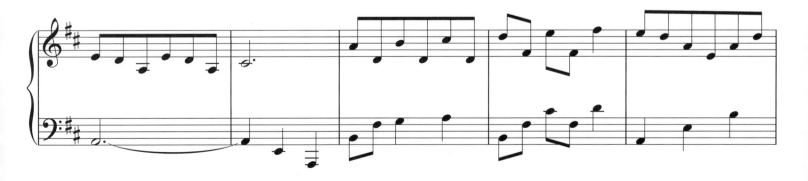

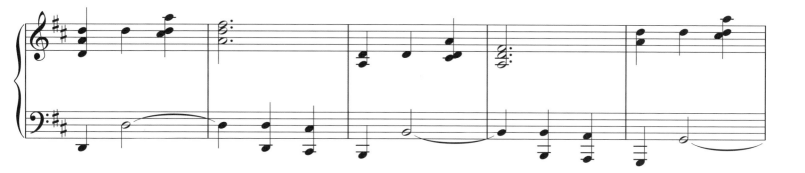

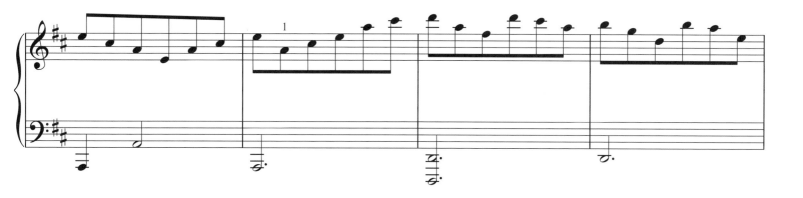

LIFT HIGH THE CROSS

Words by GEORGE W. KITCHIN
and MICHAEL R. NEWBOLT
Music by SYDNEY H. NICHOLSON

Moderately

112

Broadly

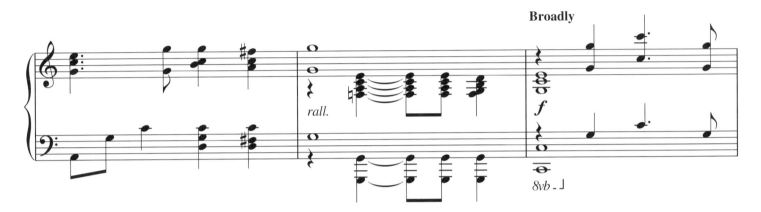

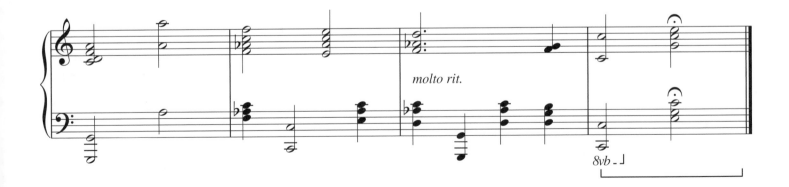